THE C...

COLLECTED AND NEW POEMS

ESSENTIAL POETS SERIES 101

Canada

Guernica Editions Inc. acknowledges the support of
The Canada Council for the Arts.
Guernica Editions Inc. acknowledges the support of
the Ontario Arts Council.
Guernica Editions Inc. acknowledges the financial support of the
Government of Canada through the Book Publishing Industry
Development Program (BPIDP).

Robert Flanagan

The Great Light Cage

Collected and New Poems

Guernica
Toronto·Buffalo·Lancaster (U.K.)
2000

In loving memory of Aileen Shattuck-Ezzy (1938-2000).

Copyright © 1970, 1972, 1978, 1990, by Robert Flanagan.
Copyright © 2000, by Robert Flanagan and Guernica Editions Inc.
All rights reserved. The use of any part of this publication, reproduced,
transmitted in any form or by any means, electronic, mechanical,
photocopying, recording or otherwise stored in a retrieval system, without
the prior consent of the publisher is an infringement of the copyright law.
Body was published in 1970 by House of Anansi.
Incisions was published in 1972 by House of Anansi.
Gravity was published in 1978 by Press Porcépic.
On the Ground was published in 1990 by Black Moss Press.

Antonio D'Alfonso, Editor
Guernica Editions Inc.
P.O. Box 117, Station P, Toronto (ON), Canada M5S 2S6
2250 Military Road, Tonawanda, N.Y. 14150-6000 U.S.A.
Gazelle, Falcon House, Queen Square, Lancaster LA1 1RN U.K.

Typeset by Selina.
Printed in Canada.

Legal Deposit – Fourth Quarter
National Library of Canada
Library of Congress Catalog Card Number: 00-107514
Canadian Cataloguing in Publication Data
Flanagan, Robert
The great light cage : collected and new poems
(Essential poets series ; 101)
ISBN 1-55071-124-5
I. Title. II. Series.
PS8561.L3G74   2000   C811'.54   C00-901166-8
PR9199.3.F56G74   2000

Contents

Body (1970) / 7
Incisions (1972) / 39
Gravity (1978) / 64
On the Ground (1990) / 85
New Poems / 118

The great light cage has broken up in the air.
                                        Elizabeth Bishop

*At the poles of eternity. When did it begin?
When did it end?*
                                        Elias Canetti

BODY
(1970)

1

Morning, the hand asleep,
beyond the night, the long night,
asleep upon the age of ledge.

Language glistening wet, the hand's eye,
in sight of peace, of entry to breathe.

Asleep, hand asleep, the night feared,
continents of lives I am waking up.
I am each skin's amaze.
I am each skin's shape of eternal.

I am stopped, searched,
seized, executed,
my name removed,
I am found years later by workmen.

I am cutting ribbons,
I am leading processions
from my mouth to my gun.

I am answered only after years of neglect,
hero, my children dashed among stone,
my arms are taut with grief.

Voice gives itself
away,
seeks the easiest way through,

cannot understand what it is saying,
carries itself badly.

Circles the block,
answers itself,
comes back for another try.

*

Begun the man,
two hands,
his face,
the extended vision,
the absolute pain,
the chant for more.

The news is now.
Two more births in the near bed.

Red at you.
I see two arms of sky.
Who kisses the body?
Who lifts the body to the skin's heaven?

In the particular row of cities
the arms held tightly to its cheek the smells
harder harder harder harder

Begun, in the way we have begun before,
with our eyes cleared of yesterday.

The cup is good.
The banal table is not banal.
Highly the pressure of now rises in the heart.
Highly and still higher we are speechless.

The animal is held in the sun's eye for resurrection.
Out of the earth the man is held transfixed in beauty.
Inside the heaven the gods sleep within the man.

Begun.
The beginning in stone.
The imprinted body in the river age.

We are near the horizon.
I see we are near the blue and yellow horizon.
We are crossing the roads.
We are armed with breath and eyes.

Begun in the now, never numb, next.

*

Begun, the man,
two hands,
his face,
the absolute pain.

Begun,
lesson 1,
he has only himself.

Begun,
his split tongue in coffee,
the tender soap of his exaltations,
the second truth.

Nothing else,
fact 3,
he counts all crimes against.

*

In my own hand, I am bleeding,
I am lung, I am tongue,
wearing my skin of eyes,
on my own tree of bones.

In my own hand, I am backward edged,
called by demons in my universe,
rolled to the blood's drum, I am
brought back to my death's grief.

In my own hand, I am led, stopped.
I am a chair, a seven.
Of me, I am ridden, kissed,
dying in my footstep, un-dead.

Essay # 1

Thoughts through discipline. It is morning. I am writing from the beginning of the beginning. The fish are very lazy here. There is very little cannibalism in our small pond. And the morning. Every day now, for the past few years, I have been very sentimental with the dawn. The language of veneer is my prerogative with blackness and blindness. And with a sun such as ours, I have no one to exaggerate its beauty. Thank god it is not as close to me as real microscopic suns.

In the beginning was the hand. It had blood. It had a beating body to recognize its own strength stretching through seconds, hours, morning, and every other important feast.

What is seen past the gun-fire? My children have died again and again in my mornings in the house where they grew past me. I have nothing to do with the earth now. My husband still lives alone, we did not succeed in bridging the chasm. Time still is killing us day by day. Sometimes I see us reflected in the usual loving lie. Other times I touch us both as we really mean to destroy our time growing old together. No delight. Nothing at all but reasons for being awake and bored.

My wife still stands by the road. We are country people here. Her branches resemble the branches of broken streams of water. We hate. Our prayers are peeled away in our waking hours together. We pray only when we are asleep. She has told me this. She sees things in the night. I don't see anything since before the last war when I saw everything clearly.

No war is news.

*

Before live witnesses,
the inward rooting takes hold.
Cement between ages,
the trembling fist filled in platitude.

Worm led, as seized in evening,
to feed the hands of love,
stupid men.

Body waits for a miracle,
eats through stones, weeds,
greets itself with a start.
Beats its chest,
caresses its earth with reluctance.

2

Morning held guard
outside the skins.
We wanted to be alone,
to watch the strange monster
by ourselves.

Our skin was the texture of communion wafers.
The minute specks of sin grew warm and fat
inside our foreheads.

Thin. We believed in thinness.

*

There is no miracle,
the sentiment turns away in disgust,
secret with self-hatred,
convinced once of miracles, anointments,
washed hands and feet,
now alone, within the heavy animal, you.

One who is flying through the air
towards the shape of memory,
out-riding death, beyond the history
of breaking, into the lightning.

Regret for all that cannot be done
by me, a birth, a boy, a man.

. . . finding out the theatre is real,
friends are not concealed before you,
but behind you. No look away, you control nothing.
I give up the war to you, the luxury of memory,
the clay army of reality, I give up the flag.

No meditation of copper burnishing, the moving body
is no meditation, it is a seeker of bodies.

. . . answer me, risen city of friends, again and again,
you are not before me, but behind me.

*

Victory exits,
city enters,
the question and answer period never seems to end,
we are sailing Tuesday again.

In the mornings snow angels quietly wept,
we were rumoured to be found in words,
but it was not true.
One of us was asleep under the moon,
another was making his manhood speech,
still another was knocking on all the doors,
as he had been doing for years, so intense he was a flame.

The truth of rain.
Alone was a truth.
Together was a truth.
Body was a continent of truths.

And then lucid drinking against time became a sacrament,
about time we cheered quietly, being believable,
and what about our personal eternity?
And our own personal angels, how do we lose them?
And our lost fashionable look, we must kill that look!
We were always very aware of our beauty.

*

Slowly, the great ships sink,
    their motors absolved of air.
    They continue their passage underwater,
    silent, huge, with the ominous grace of death.

The actors await their return,
    they look for the true story.
    Behind their masks of jade and ivory,
    the sorrow of the death of the clattering shipyards
    brings them close to the edge of the water.

The journey to the edge of the earth,
    memory, pain, temples burning.
    The eyes of the gods upon the travellers,
    the grey rain becoming like them.
    Transparent actors, waters of seduction,
    clear trembling at the peak, the sunken treasures,
    pale gold, silver, eyes, the eyes below the actors.

*

Deceived, the living recede into words,

coastal seasons drag the sea for bodies,
the empty beaches have their own beginnings.

Again. Repeated identity.
The shallow graves wail on and on.

Our maggot resists bad situations.
His cheeks touch our sex.

Again. The robbed control the absolute.
The fresh buried are solid mysteries of who and why.

*

Hush, listen close, my mouth
believes itself, so listen!
The creak of doors opening,
in the dark of black eyes,
tells the minute, jaded –
how damp in seas of ambition
your coiled wants elbow all.

I walk, my angels and devils guard me.

Time spun, I kill many animals.
The air is on fire tonight.
I torture them, again and again.

Of whom do I die of, when I kill?

I learn the world
fulfilling my ambition.

I join the skill
filling the horizon with my body,
contempt for contempt.

*

In the first,
the rude pain,
the tongue quick,
I am the century of hands.

Novice torture,
then sleeping,
then intelligence,
rooted arms, then drown.
Dull ear roar, forced appearance,

the dead knew, grew backward,
loving the needle rubber sheets.

Between dawns, circus called us home,
tiny deer knelt before the east,
silence learned of the fear of death from us.

In city stone tree arm bone
climbed from second to second,
in instant dying we.

Essay # 2

Heaven, what is a name? I am a man. My body ends in now. Travellers write me letters of remembrance. It is: the light finds nothing in my name. Unlivable.

Immensely now. Unwisely now. Nothing now. Stopped now. Birth in now. Dead in now. Sight of w, t, m, a, z.

3

Coffee, awake, wet skies,
voices safe in bed.
Watch me, wait for me this morning,
this rain of a morning,
when we believe the transformed priests,
the family blood, the full coffee pot.

Buttons off, downstairs,
her tongue catches chairs,
cups, the walls. She looks through
cupboards, unable to retreat
heavenward. Here she was
woman, girl, tongue, trembling,
feeling her skin slide down, naked.

Old tricks, the way out
of the interminable situation,
opens to whoever allows you your stupidity.

That you do not listen,
are concerned with your face.

*

She is alone,
praying well ahead of schedule.
There are times when she feels good,
feels bad.
There are times when she is saying
exactly what has to be said.
Then she is neither sad nor happy,
bad nor good, just herself,
holding out her arms,
embracing the air

The body moves
to the other room
changes skins
adjusts its history
ignores our screams
ignores our promises
doesn't remember

A home away from home
back in the ditch
under the stairs
anywhere

Marks of Cain unblemished
in the dark glowing old legends
the perfect palm
a home to be rotting within
under the insurance
against the children

Better to be sterile
to elect to suicide
than to wish for a home and property

*

Realize the real flesh
is dying
haphazard in the air

I am not a slogan
I am over there

I see away from the corners
into the lights
the food

I learn all over the beautiful
food

I am the I who dies
in the middle of dinner
allow me to apologize

I am the I who disappears
talking earnestly whichever way
I go

Standing up
surviving

*

Alone. The daily walk
from here to there.

In clear white sheets
the way home to the hard shaking
wet & accountable.

Back from the outside
to concentrate on the borders.
Trying to stop at the centre
on the way out, lover, lover.

I knew about it anyway
not the way you think
going out is dangerous
anything can go off in your hands
any possibility

. . . the hands seizing the lover,
suddenly vicious with love,

he turns into a stranger,
held against his will, he plots,
he swims away.
He hangs beneath his wounds,
twisting her toward him,
he watches the eyes always.

*

Statement of the wolf
in his plans for the future
locking the door
watching his shadow
stupid with desire
his arrogance smooth as her thighs

The leap across each
of us
how guilty
how long
how

trite
the bruise the crisis
the dramatic etc
once

Trapped
the bars soft,
going by, the perfect speech made,
the perfect act.
No ascension,
no fireworks.
Same familiar contempt for each other.
Bored, disconnected, gifts begin to be left
at certain feet.

*

Over my shoulder,
bolder than ever,
you stalk my walks,
around this room,
as if you know me,
as if I wanted to know you.
The steps the only reality, eh?

Hidden, the nightmare ends.
Endless room after room
empty of space, packed with jokes.
Out of the hidden corners
come old friends, intent.

Calming cigarettes, the frozen radio,
walking across the mouths of the seconds.
Here hiding, within each skid,
cleaning the sink, watching the clock.

Exploration of a cage
the cavity between

tragedy

in the exactitude of each lock's depth

*

The hidden language,
you smile,
you laugh out,
tea and whispers of eyes,
how are you?
Cigarettes, friends, rooms,
the hidden language,
how are you?

Essay # 3

The actors must be brought before themselves somehow. They must be confronted with themselves whenever possible. The walking must become meaningful to them. The directions must contain their whole spirits. The actors must be conscious of their movements. The actors must be conscious of what is possible. They must think like themselves. When they are alone and no one can see them, they must still be aware of what they are part of, of who they are.

*

Intent on interior
the body focussing on itself
slowly standing alone

Alone
going through the air
riding the swelling there

4

Day forth, the formula,
skinned man hung,
hunger tired in his sleep,
am necessary I, you.

Be nights alone, loose head,
find reason to climb down jaws of animal normal nothing.

*

Spat on man,
began the inner ear,
loved the embrace,
killed the embrace.

He walked to the cupboard,
poured himself a child,
looked for a gun.

Blood must be shown.

Blood must be shown.
Weapons are to be used.

Every clock is to be smashed.

We will wake the killers.
We will wake the fires.

Bodies will be symbols once again.

Essay # 4

One is conscious of dying. Of dying alive. The air is no longer breathable. The charade is horrifying in its utter rapacity for continuation above all else.

It is the careful lies to lovers.

We die. We leave. We arrive somewhere else. We separate the grafted skin. Or else what?

Essay # 5

That I am the man who is ignorant of cruelty. That I am the man who caresses the machine. That I am the man who produces & asks no questions. That I am the man who strikes like a cobra & is proud of his prowess. That I am seen through & used. That I am the man who walks away from the pain.

*

Apparatus of the machines,
at the foot of the body,
singing the machine ways softly.

The apparatus of the machines
listens to the crippled with splendid pain
of awareness,
holding us with tender voltage.

*

Freedom is hung
in the window
advertising the infinite wares
of justice
of public good
for all who pass
the bullet-shattered glass

In my century
the bones have conspired
to remain

In praise of the universal horror
in dutiful homage to the universal mistake
I take this moment in all history
to congratulate the dead the living the unborn
for being the animals of true death of true birth
in leaping across time without thought
in seizing control of the heavy future in
anger

Montreal

Mustaches are heavier now. Everyone is leaving the city or learning how to use a gun. You learn survival habits up close to the last drink.

The mountain is when you climb up the steps looking at the ducks in the pond with revolution in their eyes.

City of the St. Joseph.
Blood of the Metropole kiss.
Yards full of hoops and iron bars.
War-eye country.

*

Morning, bloody Sunday,
the tables are turned,
everyone is a general.
We are running into roadblocks,
we are calling for the time.
Then we are dead
Then we are found too late.
Then we are caught up to our necks.

Morning, bloody Sunday,
the knowledge of the world.
The pure, sparse, temple light.
The rumour of last judgement.
The rumour of first judgement.
Weapons are discovered,
shots are heard three streets away,
have we any food left?

That I lived in the dream of the real city
in the body of my life.

That the real city grew within me
obsessed with its magnificence.

That the real city appeared pure
& monumental against all flesh.

Knelt fire made in dust,
I am leading no one
away, am I?

*

The lights go out,
pause, weeds grow
past the skyscrapers,
pause, let me smash your pedestal, pause,
let you know that I won't build
another one, pause.

Mother can you hear

The revolution is yours

Aged in meals

Apart

Mother of the birthday of the hollow eyes
I am descending upwards

Mother can you hear

Plant the seed
destroy the outline
fill in with vegetable mineral human –

Overflows its roots
spills the colour of the earth
strains the conversation into all direction –
Kill the legend of perfections –

Walk of the unknown soldier
is to blow up the damn statue –

*

My killing human, I
break through enough,
know the street, morning,
laughter, gunfire,
entrance to weeping,
going in the body
past the steel shells, under
mouth, to bone.

5

. . . the first century blooms again,
the fresh red paint is scarcely dry,
holy communion is received in white uniforms,
have years, we have cried forever,
alive in the blue fish painting of each other.

Sleep, all the children are sleeping.

For Shelly

Near the harbour, the mountain,
the children are dancing,
in the snow, the beds go dreaming,
ago, bless with hand, with sun,
the good bread game. Near the melting snow,
with orange and sky, the command of air,
go slow with arms outside the fire,
holding the wind in open palm, go well.

*

Through night alone,
the children go,
into foreheads.
The arms outstretching earths,
breaking the final secret second,
in slow yellow afternoons,
across the endless yards.

For Shelly

Sun fall these shells
slide down the beach,
past my clawed arms,
back into the ocean's strength.

Ocean fall these hours.
The stopping clocks, one by one,
drift off to sleep, arms
together by choice, no alarms.

You fall these bodies
are you – free, past,
present, future, called into
the sun, the ocean, the body worlds.

The poor, the rim of the eye,
are not disparate,
the spectrum of pain.

Distended, the conjecture of love,
intelligible,
one hour.

I Brought Her None

Did the sea break under her
in the early early morning time?

Did I bring her anything
in the yawn of love?

Dance begins, enter me sweetly,
the birthday of hands,
the last jazz a.m. along you,
through the intimate corners,
across the wide open bodies,
the heroes begin again and again.

My love she sings the night down
under my eyes she sleeps uneasily
in her way   in her way

My love walks beyond words
into dangerous space
body before body

My love

*

My mouth   your mouth
snow drifts
into the clearing

East & arrival
at the mouth

Nailing me against the bed
fade back

Sing me to sleep
ride me awake
Easy lover

*

Bare bone me,
seek me below shoulders,
under my days, touch me here.

Sing my hours alone,
bare all my truth for me,
take me alive,
love me.

*

. . . done then, the art of love,
the actors spent,
the ordinary night,
arteries ago, the ages of bodies bled.
The performance through love, hate,
fire, water, bodies of sand, stone.
Done then, they go to morning,
alone, asleep, apart, now.

6

Sleep   sleep
sleep is at an ending

We dry the morning air
with great eyes full of plans

In the going out of our listening
into our bodies singing

Sleep   sleep
sleep is at an ending

. . . said again, in a darkness,
let us leave in our own time,
whole, intact, unbroken,
open.

This island pledged beyond the scent of sea,
bare arms, bare clearing, a place to continue
the language of skin, of eyes.

. . . said again, begin, break the circles,
chalk the drum with flesh,
allow, allow, allow.

*

All night long, snow fell.
Witches fled the earth,
singing of blue fingers,
blue hair, blue bodies,
of the lovers who rode the night
soundless through the falling snow.
Where I go through this air,

I am found in mornings, explored, full,
eternity in my fingers, my hair,
my body. Barely the morning rose through the lovers,
naked days, free,
I know, I know,
we founding we.

A stone through the head,
a mouth of eyes,
drops of rain in the hand,
I am, I am.

The storm loud,
louder than I am.
Finding the air alive inside the
man who
clings,
yells ahead.

That I am the red-eyed fox who eats
his food alone
who eats the black space between the white bones

That I am the fox who moves away
from the river back across the meadow
into the bushes tongue hanging fur dripping

*

The claws are debating,
the witches burn brighter,
it is time to end drama.

We must have room to live inside animals.
Blood buries.
Exhibit A is the right answer.

The land-animals follow
the direction of the outrageous.

Turning earth,
spat on man,
kill the child.

Belief same,
anchors fed,
sanity alive, led, coward.

*

The air with its pulse grew,
the tongue curled around the days
of the body.

The skin grew.

Between trees the body is stretched,
is split,
towards the sky,
away from the earth,
taut with consciousness.

The hollowness expressed,
the leaping from log to log,
slipping in the rain,
squatting on the shore-line cleaning the fish.

The body severed from itself.
The mouth of the fish full of blood.
The scales sticking on the fingers, body
smothered in butter, thrown into the frying pan.

The body expressed,
the hollowness filled with bones,
under the sky,
nada in the goodness.

The jar of the body
was filled with water,
fish were added,
entrails fed to them,
mouths of the sins.

The body in the air,
smashing on the rocks,
the fish moving in the grass,
the water drying in the sunlight.

*

I shall live on the beach

The mountains above me
the ocean below me

I shall grow in the consciousness of the air
I shall not be alive alone

The sky
the water
the rock
the fish
the sky

I shall live on the beach

I am seeking the way through the sweat,
into the build-up of careful incisions.

I am recognizable to myself.

Find me the word that buries the mountains.
Bless me with silence.

Body power
wrong

In the pain of human size

in the strain of maintaining the dead

*

Animal days,
the air clean,
the water clear,
the honest rewarded with freedom.

No promises!

An apple, a sun-clock, a parable, a tiger,
a lion, a bear.

7

Morning, the hand asleep,
beyond the night, the long night,
asleep upon the age of ledge.

Language glistening wet, the hand's eye,
in sight of peace, of entry to breathe.

Asleep, hand asleep, the night feared,
continents of lives I am waking up.
I am each skin's amaze.
I am each skin's shape of eternal.

INCISIONS
(1972)

1

I am here,
I live, I live.

I wake, I wake,
I take notice.

I begin.
I stop.

I seize,
I seize again.

*

I an identity
a business mouth

that departs
at the wink of an eye

in hope of getting
the necessary supplies

*

I guard the one true entrance
the one true exit
I ascend
to the exchange of goods

*

This I,
a face,
a location,
a compass of bone.

Precise,
made out of parts,
found at the mouth of a river.

*

Incisions
where I hide & sleep
ride & keep

I deceive,
answer half-listening

*

Begun in the instant,
moving with the speed of an honest man
into the lap of morality,
my body stages its celebrated uprising.

I stand on my own,
for a minute or two.

*

Simplification of justice:
I am stronger,
I shall live longer.

Waking to the familiar,
waiting for the opening,
walking to the door.

*

Fear
as I break arms

keeping a grip on method
I bow to the ceiling

*

I wake to imperfection
in the mouth of the pain
no one saw me leave
no one saw me come back in

I am invisible
as I wanted always
to be

Everything moves according
to my laws
I see what I want to see

*

Seas erupt,
telephones go dead.
Working the entrance wider
I vanish into the mouth of history.

Turning corners
I am fed by coercion.

I am timed at regular intervals,
an immediate sarcasm.

*

The self imploded,
harboured by what is believed.

Allowing blood to boil,
calcifying bones to sleeplessness.

Moment of hand-shakes,
harsh sunlight hanging over the myths.

In return, attempting to break
through solid walls.

*

To the side,
razor-led days.

Observer beside solution,
memory short-lived,
pitching forward.
Ambition
happy with its fate.
Ice-snake
gliding from level to level.

*

These cold arches of living,
proud as any beauty,
the breath believed as the only wonder.

Opaqueness of the image,
holding casually who I want to remember,
re-enforcing who I am.

*

Again the importance of interior drawing,
Again the lunging, who painted this wall?
Who made excellent colour?

This colour swelling my body.

*

Declaring done,
I sat within nothing,
alone with skin,
the death-skin.

Nothing said, as spiders
stopped in the street,
to weave my dead skin
to the blue sky.

*

A chase,
universe above,
horizon thriving on what is.

Solitary parent,
earth below,
greed I have in abundance.

Tongue I am,
distance intact,
out of mind into mind.

*

Exploration of a testing ground,
from knowing to not understanding.

The skin an awareness of collapse,
calling the seconds to stop.

Seeing what else?

*

Place of hospital,
impotent rage

lists of faith
shoved in your face

empty plain
cathedral of brochures

two rivers,
one racing from me
the other towards me

*

Eulogy of spite,
at the attic's mouth.

After identity is made,
where to stay?
Where to go?

Ascension inside the skull,
waiting for answers.

*

Heightened by generalities
I do not want to see
what I see

A fate of living
feet in the air
the internment of differences

*

Old of my old
where I am
when I am called old

Frightening the body
toward that room
where I am observer only

*

Perishable hands in the search
where the seasons are bare

beyond the intent of honour
in the rigid memory of where

by a field of the body
anguished in its force

I am the human

*

The body
ends
with the presence of skin

detaching the who
from the I

*

Lord above, the look
is suspicious, closed.
I can not see anyone.

My breakage of idols is continuous.
My breakage of myself is continuous.

2

Time of suspension
systematic blunt hammer
friend of the poor
enemy of the poor
fact defying fact
element of play
intensity of hope beyond confrontation

*

Ourselves
we declared beyond our culture
ultra-real before each other

Days of wish
future before us
ignorant as sharks

*

Out of you,
out of me,
an energetic stupidity,
with memory,
with fear.

*

Pure ego,
the devil's due.

At the beginning of experience
a shrine is calculated.
Behind the skin,
a mirror.

*

Totem sang
harpoon lied
man tied
fist to blister
blister to rumour

Miracle of will
armful of eels
tip of the iceberg
work   walls   tables
iron in dominance

*

Mineral hope,
in the exact price on head,
balancing the squeeze with belief.

Tongue, clock, space,
explicit use.

*

The man
must not be trusted.

Alone
he is frightened by the darkness.

With each ordinary day
he is mistaken for a god.

*

Fear the man
who hates,
he has leaders.

Despair of the man
who controls his fate,
he is an example.

*

Clumsy exile,
food & shelter.

Can you dance?
Can you cope?

What do you see?
What do you hope?

*

Creature-kiss,
what is manipulated in the law winks.

Brain, eye, pride,
violins play on.

Familiar street, faces,
the glove fits.

Salt, vinegar, bread,
one day through the next.

*

Intensity of definition,
not wanting nearness,
but answers.

War,
lucifer tree,
oasis of firm directives.

*

If necessary
interior shots
widened
to fit

One two
what to do
steps whistling
in the news

*

In the distances
the world seemed

an arena
a spot of blood

single-filed
straight & true

*

Weeping the wicked
starving the fool
alive to deed

Interior bug
tricking blood
finalized in sweat

*

Lesson on,
black-suited surety,
Christ of the weep,
pedant's triumph,
bruises within arms,
this living.

Feverish hands,
the water of sticks drying
in locked, close quarters.

*

Trying to leave,
stay.

Of the world, not
of this world, existing
side by side.

Isolation by consent,
toward noon, midnight,
apex of coming, going.

*

Bending to curve the man,
drops of dying tighten
his belt, open doors & windows
in the underwater pressure.

Water streaming to the ground.

*

Clearly we die
one cannot remain

Clearly into ourselves
& out the other side

Clearly we are laconic
one cannot remain

*

Death's wand
the seeing sky

Memory's delight
eternal shore-line

A mouthful of beliefs
the affliction of exits

*

Sardonic dancer
held to the eye without mercy

In the narrow way out of here
stepping towards an unclear end

*

Into another dimension of excitement
a slow turning
beneath the surface

The intent of becoming visible
against arbitrary decay

Conscious continuous

*

Understand what you witness
what you must do

Stop the angel search
feed the man

Disperse the wealth
grow lean

3

Hours go
over the moon
under the lips

Aware of the skin's
flight over

*

Totem & smoke
speak to her

In her hair
rabbit bone
deer antler

*

What begins is four-footed,
stiffened to the wall.

Under the external skin a system
of signals, of underground necessities,
a devotional waterfall of location.

*

Open as despair
out of reach
elements collide

Voice to voice
flesh to flesh
growing through pursuit

*

It sobers me
when I am on the same street
with you.

I don't forget our similarities
for a minute.

*

How we forgive
heavy-handed into mist
watching the sky disappear

Through each embrace
discovering the warm breast
wanting the minutes to extend

*

An event,
living out the essential drama
between each other without hesitation.

A smile,
each understanding more intimate.

*

Passion
with a sense
of finality
begins its
peacock destiny

*

Intent
between tongue
& thigh

Inside the body
a seeing eye

*

A kiss
that drives home
its message
with the delicious flavour
of dominance
over dominance

*

Without comment
watching
the sun
enter the room
intent on confrontation

*

Rhetoric of bees
rain on the rug
looking out windows down at the street

In the midst of prints
the body moving in & out
of its persona

*

In the bed's length
the hairs of morning
stroke our cheeks

Sunlight robber
of the orchard of night

Delight in the sound
of the water street cleaner

*

Symmetry of dream,
breath relaxed.

A peak,
tongue on the vine.

Open field.
Turned around.

*

She is one seen second
on the eyelid
formed in the art of becoming

She is before me
as one day is here seen seeing

In the mouth's search
I am the lover
on that curve of skin
within her

*

Love is translucent.

In this search
we are its proof,
the other premise.

We remain astonished.

*

Conception of being eternal
within the immediate release of being

Drawn toward the shape of things
to come

Abstract held aloft

*

In fear's pleasure,
old before they are young,
lovers embrace the beginning of life.
Bearing gifts of arms, lips, care,
exploring each other,
again & again, as if forever.

*

In the confident relief
of the horizontal situation,
lovers see the eternal,
revere the premise,
drown the world,
attempt to dominate
at least one other.

*

To the sea-foam house,
(a consummate swan-dive
the correct cast of light
handshakes all round),
come the lyrical cynics
giving orders with the intensity
of completing a landscape

*

It is a pleasure
for perfect love
blissful check-mates
to help flights
across this room
burdened by unexpected life
in the corners

*

Head in a sling,
jabbing between ribs,
into what?

Out of this skin into what skin?

An agreement to allow space?
Into one from two?

A litter?
Carbonization of a friendship?

*

I am not tired enough
to let go
of what did occur

What did occur
was a peace
I still do not understand

*

Enough is broken
weapons damned
stone entry
Strangely find time spent
time-watch
clear crystal
rain without a difference

*

Words apart,
we see the body
as we see each other.

First we break through,
then we stop.

*

Soaked in lime
treating the bed
with respectable misery

Ladders locked
theatre of two
spending time

*

A trance
needing existence as one

Wrestling the demons
to the sound of heads cracking
The order of curses
bruised lips

*

Flint to rock,
monuments under the skin,
time devours roots,
shovels up feet first,
grows cracks in the floor,
asserts identity.

*

To endure a signal
of cunning,
sound within reach,
absolute man, woman, god.

Not a stone left unlearned,
departure with tears,
logic of sky, earth, self.

*

Yes & no
centre of being
bridge of flesh

The sudden stops & leaps
sun in the hand
going with you as you go

GRAVITY
(1978)

Directives/Realizations

Begat from when?
Out of what arrogance?

A circle of o's on the forehead
between birth & funeral day.

I am gate & exit
Into & out of attacks, retreats.

What I say, I am.
What I do, I am.

*

Staring equation
featured egg
shot out of the evening bush.

Angel's flight
races across pools of light.

My conduct assertive
sinner hooded.

*

God-haunted
I pass the mist.

On time for the next

I am dead to this world.

Strained from below
I catch my own weight.

Compulsive grin
I mix my dosage of glue.

*

Impact of yes prisoner
I eat mirror-packed universe
play both sides of the fence.

I fear eternal pain
split hairs
make dogma from ritual.

I seal questions
I agree
I live a measure-suited day.

Poverty of nodding optimism
I deal in withdrawal
a manager clumsy with his keys.

Manager mud-kingdom
property of drains
I ritualize sceptic.

*

Inside an impudent first step,
preacher of facts,
I stayed between house & school.

Nowhere be well –
mysterious fingers are turning the earth
upside down!

Security worshipped,
hands trailing in water,
defenceless man is alarmed.

Drool dreaming years,
sleeper lurching in the dark,
a wrinkled anxiety, a fear of dying.

*

Spit in his eye
past the conscious eye –

Record this refusal to obey you,
the paternal god.

*

My own glib interior, my opportunist,
ass over fire,
is between now & then, first & last.

Puritan with squirming pillow,
shove of exalted momentum,
old age flattens ahead.

Longer than he attends,
I want reward for my anger at being.

*

I am thrown over the side
to sink, swim,
worry at absolute bite.

Learning nerve
I accept my vanishing point.

It is good to see you
kicking myself without hesitation.

Calm intervals reflect my purity.

Direct assault, defiance,
I am the malignant driver
before I have stopped using this body.

*

Worm's grin
opposition to corruption.

Comic & otherwise
I classify my appetite for visibility.

This & more.

Pushed to earth.
Brain to wish.

*

Cynical bird,
educated in warfare,
remarkable with gravity.

Attentive symbols,
for each resemblance
the hours I know.

Growth of an endless sentence,
noun of nouns,
perched on the back.

*

Mother rocks a
thin-skinned complainer.

Tabled birth,
dexterity to belong,
launched by the animated utensils.

Surplus expected,
I the relation, talk,
crawl, walk, out of family.

*

On the road to complete description, I think about
    ways
to out-fox death, as if that changes results.

I have lost myself within this arbitrary decay.

As if there is another side, I land on both feet.

I cross over in the stapled ease of my nerve-ends,
    dead.

Street Addict's Condition

Over & done with,
enemies remembered,
lists to keep.

Active persecution,
whom to fight?

Dry as dust,
I wait in the street.

*

Emergence of a history
bought & sold.

Trailed free man
looks over his shoulder.

He is suspicious,
stopped on sidewalk.

Here he is –
picking at his spine.

*

Humid & dry
restaurant wisdom is wired on.

Righteous bruise is
watched & out of power.

Talk of enemies of the food,
resources of ownership,
threats to a meal.
Clarity of place –
a self-conscious leap is
led through the monologues.

*

By expansive conceits of revery,
fish shadow a lake with grace.

I run two dogs.
Ship out to sea.

Smoke drifts from the hand-made pipe,
seven/eleven on dice.

Moved to intimacy & release,
I am part of a melted clock.

*

Inert sense
defined as stick,
a street shaman hangs on.

Quick getaways,
the run,
stood up to wall,
dragged out of drum.

Dues & flesh, one end.
Closed eyes, mouth, suit.

*

Police arrive,
light switched on,
being arrested
in front of the gun.

Pace with a morality
of sorts –

Not answered, but ignored,
endured.

*

Sailing into sight,
poise is entertained away
from the curb.

I visit the popular dead:
comfort, a parallel development.

Rush is tongued,
absorbed in a face
esteemed in the singular.

Awake, asleep,
night of crowds,
the police settle down.

*

Woman rakes the cut grass,
mountains at billowing blue curtains.

Summer stretches like a cat
through clear mornings,
children playing on the lawn.

Rain in an afternoon,
I push my fingers along the iron
railing, balcony wet.

*

Winners project
splashing through hot water.

Losers project
feeling along open raw wounds.

Lucid compulsions project
linking up-front killers.

Passive/active hostility,
maintenance fixates the good citizens.

*

A self-imposed contest
enforcing the laws of decay.

To sink back,
the desire to sink back.

Men watching the horizon.

*

A fool for sore salvation
stairways to heaven are dismantled.

Trees in random time
shake their roots.

Smell of a fix
up against the winking eye.

With vigorous intent
this believer scuttles
across an indifferent sediment.

*

Mechanical with the individual, ethical with the corporate power, art of Leader is to manipulate with exact timing.

Leader organizes his supporters in disciplined units. He provides what hasn't been wrapped.

As actors we proceed with the convention. The production is convincing. We are convinced & moved into definite decisions or we lose.

Worm in convulsions, action snakes across the convention floor. Posters look for new walls to conquer. Theatre of mouth shouts.

*

Hope – art of seduction
dissolves into sheets, blankets.

Heaving bed, ticking heart,
structure is punctuated with the bills paid.
Muscular interest,
routine is aware of the lawful submission.

Naive, this fabric snaps
at its own leash.

Coming & Going

Celebrated arrival
friend at a door.

Love's exhaustion
leaf on a floor.

Love's estate
love's weather
impulse spent, measured.

*

Volcano pose
a smile
the control.

Through a cultivation of gesture,
roses, roses, everywhere.

Staged on a slippery mat,
nights against her elbow.

*

Forgiveness
toward the other,
passing from loathing
to caress.

Insight
part of spite,
this mismatch
needs our polarity.

*

Bits of bread,
exterior shots of a game,
I walk to the second creek,
dog barking at ground-hogs.

Sower of fields,
fields drenched with rain,
dead-pan tongues lick their sores
as tedious as this August.

*

Habits of refusal,
in the evidence
traced to passivity.

At the farm
locked in a slow
falling arc.

Box within smaller box,
built from corners,
isolation.

*

Immortal chamber
ceiling of clouds
where the wood groans.

Surrounded by exit routes
interlude of remorse.

*

Wide-awake
between pretensions
we ate.

belly slapped
blinking lids
energy to praise.

You & I
parts to feast
rubbed by the dollars.

*

Precise angle
ideal sand chased through the wait.

Blunt instruments, salt-sweat,
erotic dream expressed.

Bird dance
carried over to resolute orgasm.

Animals intent
accomplished in countdown.

Skill by boredom, an
appearance made with a shape
of this other, a command
with the strut of town-criers.

*

Living up to this date
through the woods
kneeling on hot wind
working up to the city gates
waiting for current vacuum
to collapse oak beams
these exhilarated occupants

*

Dialogue progresses
from a plateau
of careful observation.

Tanned skin
comes in lamplight
across a dark gold bed-spread.

Certain agreements,
some clouds, trees,
use this summer breeze.

*

Erect pronoun ready,
I follow you across the words,
breathless with ambition.

O hungry salutations to the sinking expansion
of appetite & wit!
New car in the ravine,
hard shot to the head,
we collaborators of the expanded conscious
    melodrama.

*

A consumer.
The consumed.

Not ourselves
taken in surprise
but our bodies blessed by experts
at balance.

Screen to fine screen –
hall light singing a cynic's lament –
doubtful roles, then doubts,
then roles, then roles.

*

Sky, affection.

Between straight lines
what is known is memory.

Delirium of the achieved centipede
I remember the entrance
inside methodical her.

Twist in my pocket.

Dry ice,
watching he/she
evaporate in this bed.

At moments when it is
possible to start,
the man, the woman, turn their backs.

*

Face is devil, bled again.
Blood's ring is on fire.

Able to fall back through the pores,
satisfy the crazy.

*

Here we are
being drawn away

Textured life
held in particular

the air alive
as you & I.

*

A plan not realized
on expectation of change.

Wife & husband
elaborate, exhausted with the familiar.

Gauntlet. Hot to cold.
A calculation of emotions.

Dried apples
moon on the road
we meet.
The way the memory of how
it is easier to break.

*

Inside an expected net
we writhe & jump identities.

The two created
lead us for miles.

Any action to be is praised.

Praise aggression, womb.

As we finish we bargain.

*

This foot dreams home
floating acclaimed hole.

Deliberate with nostrils
swearing torso climbs up.

Happy front face
rim of earth –
arms alert from lifting, setting down.

*

In the present
tunnelling a maze.

Sprawling kisses
inside cliche.

Quarry drawn out
avidity of the hunt.

*

Determined kiss on your neck,
fingers on belt,
the next active wave,
follow me, follow me.

These days we walk in a
perfection of smoothness,
appointing bodies
all the time, all the time.

*

Love's heat
suggestion of eternity.

Hooves of a colt
hands in a river
cupping cold water.

Love's heat
suggestion of horns.

Strength of the bull
waiting for no one
having been found.

*

Love, love,
in the soup
containing calm argument.

At the source
a pride in self-possession.

Free-fall of opening
not there in the abstract,
but here.

ON THE GROUND
(1990)

That Was Then

That was then. You
returned to a single
image. A touch of snow.
In contrast with. Change
it. Change it. He said
he didn't expect to live
to fifty. Yes, I stayed
longer. Seriously. First
class. Living winter.
She said near by. Affection
of looking at things.

From Things Themselves

From things themselves. Because
you think of it doesn't make it
true. Tree-branches signalling
in front of the windows. Colder.
The dead beside table. An intense
& elevated sensuality. We skate
to the next village. Past & away.

I Go

I go from one thing to
another. Revenge. All
kinds of cameras. Otherwise,
a long sleep. Apparent
repetition. Not to sustain.
For a few days. We are very
worried. & by that time.
Had no wish to hide.
Move ahead.

What Is

What is experienced &
accepted. First discovered
in open space. Those who
had been there were talking.
Our decisions. A gradual
saddening within much
activity. On a scrap of
paper. No god forbid.

The Pine-cone on the Bridge Table

The pine-cone on the bridge table.
To do with a fence. It belonged
to father. A stubborn naturalist.
I know what happens. While you
grow older. To go beyond playing
the game. Would no longer speak to
other players. We made out a list.
It must mean you have occurred.

Structure with the Living

Structure with the living.
Build a perfect stairwell to
a past. Justification in the
view of a city. Not a dog
in sight. Gates of Paradise.
Even if it contradicts the work
itself. A surprised look. Fresh
bread. This interaction, these
phenomena. Avid disinformation
of the limbs.

Gate of Restraint

Gate of restraint.
His important drum solo
insists. Lonely grenade
explodes every pore. Savage
island drowns. Head swells
dumb-bell anger. She jolts
him. Rocket ride up Amazon. A
fin rests on wet shore.

Ah, It's Rich

Ah, it's rich, it's elegant,
ghosts slip by, always
the past, a view from a cab
window, cozy in the snow-storm.
An interval of property
owned, work finished, humid
shirt to dry, playing, always
playing. Coughing, not at play,
but in a hospital.

There Are Other Places

There are other places. You
are right. Past displayed.
We sit drinking whiskey under
the sea. Venerable puddles in the
manner of Duke Ellington. Up
& down our streets we drive.
I want to play the slot-machines.
Wet shoes in mud April.

Law & Order

Law & order. Good legal
cement. A bourgeois
prudence with bathrooms.
Stand up & be myth. We didn't
know what was going to happen.
Hoof-beats across the valley
of heart-attacks. Patriotic
boulders of destiny. Huge
snails. Authority by extremely
modern condominium.

That's Why People

That's why people need to take
up logic. A certain set of
relationships. I want happiness
& goodness. & you never responded?
Who you are not. He wasn't finished.
On my head here. She has a pretty
face. The expressive quality of
colour in an entirely new manner.
Certain field of grass in spring.

River Night

River night. Chairs
squeak. Heads sway
to the music. Tree-tops
rustle in our heads. Energy
solar. Furniture burns on
chemical future. Bee-stings
of ideal dishes. This town
predicts more barking.

No Not Cancer

for my father

No not cancer
as himself –
rather, raiment
of skull dance
in his face.

Torso test.
Worn indoor road he's on.

Confused & distanced.
Pinch him!

Dying: loud radio,
singing old man,
nurse shouting your name,
hand to the catheter,
leg over the edge.

Hole in sky.

Shuddering man,
daylight, pleasurable,
wavering, world. O no.

Of Her Disappearance

Of her disappearance. Had not
mastered the method. Afternoons
still warm. Bred to believe in.
While kissing her. Fascinated by
the tools. For all these reasons.
Never compromised. Comic changes.
Has character. It seemed to me.

One Thing or the Other

One thing or the other. The
orbit of the earth. The path
of the sun. The lawn-chair
beneath the plum-tree. The
iron gate. Your shoulder-blade.
Concrete expression of morning.
A small starting salary. I've
got to get into there. At this
time. Our mental life. If I
had the money. They like my
work. It draws you in. Something
broke free. She's given in to
reality, to tragedy. That made a
lot of sense to me. History with
a softer focus. To make them alike.

Mind at You

Mind at you as
radiant dead. Not
dead but love. Dead-safe
in lazy midnight
smoke. Moral breasts
taken under game. Ashes
in jealous, galloping bar.
Acrobats on the piano.
Aggression of belief. Snow
brushed face. Stronger than
before. As other.

The New Season

The new season. Destroy
tight corners. Sound
of painting. Properly fed
& dressed for dessert.
Sincerity of hallucinations.
Found odd things, reasons
for primitive behaviour by
millionaires. Disobeying
a court injunction. A deep
impression. Frequent & prolonged
holidays. Had put his lunch.

Baby at Breast

Baby at breast. We're open late.
What it should be & isn't. Sexual
schemes. The mentioning of streets
& cars. In that city of music,
the future of beauty. You are
recalling the pictures of your
existence. The shape of an individual.
What do we discover instead? Why
do we live? Where historians stop.

They Pursued It

They pursued it without
relaxation. Some coral
shrubs. Absence of a friend's
voice. A new menu. Energetic
woman ironing in a laundry window.
A sonorous agitation through
the school years. By the brush
of some Flemish artist. Transfigured
night. She bounces the ball against wall.

In a Thoughtless Moment

In a thoughtless moment agreed
to a deal. Artificial energy.
Older slopes, voices. Got away
with it. She didn't work hard
at domestic chores. A gift of garden
vegetables. Nothing matters. A
serious question. I stopped &
listened to the companion. At
that time of the day. In dubious
taste. Easy & gleeful.

But No

But no. Yes was happiest
sweeping the sand. Snow
on the lake in the sunlight.
You travelled with great humour.
You did a little excerpt on tv.
What a sad story. Less of a
revolutionary force. Worshipping
the ancestors. With the proud
romantics. There is the good suit.

By the Minute

By the minute as people.
Or some other day. The
experienced. Rude hotel-room.
Significant systems. A
state of rebellion. Construct
the sidewalk. Student of law.
Devil the tenant. The weather.
Discovering more information.
Cherish the hardest test. I
am ashamed. An explanation is
being produced.

He Wasn't Finished

He wasn't finished. We
wanted to go home. Your
private work. The newer
decades. So we had one.
If I was in the desert.
So different from me.
It's just a tiny step.
Become available. Accept
what happens. Which was
most of the time. I mean
about frustration.

Were Not Issued Permits

Were not issued permits to
stay. Back-to-work signal.
Summer leaves. Field on
fire. The incident put him
in the hands of a hangman.
Even that movie has its place.
Resignation of a creator.
Every creature dies. The idea
of a map. At a table drinking
coffee. Specialist's attitude.

Being Attentive

Being attentive. We drank
on the plane. The dark you
can touch. That's not easy.
She loved news at all. Came
into the lens. On reading.
I didn't like the party. A
rug you washed. Meaningful
conversation surprised by the
lack of pleasure. As we are
enjoyed. They laugh.

They Drifted

They drifted a few
leagues down river.
More to follow. internal
wars are responsible. Cult
of genius. Final liberation
at the ranch. People who
lived there spoke favourably
of a disgraced minister. He
sat in his truck with a cigarette
in his mouth. He would live for
a number of years. She is bounded
by accessible mountains.

The Tribe of Optimists

The tribe of optimists. A
more intimate examination. To
be consistent. The balloon
on a floor. Don't you prefer?
I have concentrated on the
important merchants. When the
cliches ended I was at work.
I expressed a naive view of my
country. Inclined towards comfort.
Yes & no. At a glance, the museums.

This Is a Money Sky

This is a money sky. Hot &
cloudy. Candid hamburger
wisdom of money. The car door
is too healthy. This is an
ignorant friend, a professional
neighbour. They want a guarantee
of seriousness. Insurance & doctors
& children are icons – props of
repeated gestures in smoking piles
of leaves.

So Calculated

So calculated. Walking through
the complex, we blushed with
representation. Cold wind outside.
The battery is alive. What matters.
The new pants matter. They too are
my puppets. Long talks with happy,
noisy, she.

The Next Moment

The next moment. Years of
after experience. Where it
is moving. Out there. His
illusions. Moral routines.
A dreamlike memory. Several
minutes in the memory. &
denounce the district of judges.

While Working Outdoors

While working outdoors. Continuous
erratic light. The last autumn.
Tied to the clouds. The water a
colour of leaf. In pity. In their
usual path. Full of splendid characters.
Courage into the grave. For a
considerable time. A copy of their
requests. Left open in a smile.

All that Remains Is Joy

All that remains is joy.
Painter shows her paintings. The
attitude of their heads. Correct
response. A charming thing &
full of taste. More complete
than an orchestra. To be miserable
& in heat. In the earthly
paradise of this period. We are not
an earlier phase of liberation.

Situated

Situated by solemn
children of summer,
white-washed walls,
courtyard pecked by
sensible birds – I
live as sovereign state.
Don't fail. Don't fall up.

Often He Forgets

Often he forgets. Only through
the word. Cream of the cream.
An indifferent city to premonitions.
Gratitude is pleasing. Fall
fair of traffic on a curving highway.
Sad child at night before the blankets.
But this is a high note.

Memory. Time. Nostalgia.

Memory. Time. Nostalgia. In
the name of love. Fear of
running into them. To wait
alone. She gathers fear every
day. Objects of their aspirations.
Pictures on a floor. Radical
visions. In the weeks that followed
interpretations. Stood by themselves.
Hold it. Sufficient number of
experiences. Almost nothing. Inside,
more light.

A Look of Permanence

A look of permanence. The
individual's love of self.
New glass doors. Weeping
behind shuttered windows.
It is wind unable to sleep.
My grease mark. Unimportant
servant. Secrets cluster in
the corridor. We are trying
to repeat to preserve.

Reassuring Those

Reassuring those in the know.
Given elements of the body.
Voice of death. You said so.
Insistent geometry. Cat in her
hair. The flesh, that proud
nation, declares independence.
Bank called. Holy real estate.
She walked with her head down.
His personal behaviour set a bad
example. Ground cool.

Painting Is Just a Sign

Painting is just a sign.
Happiness changes clothes.
What other explanation except
fashion? Ghost shouts memory.
You bought it, you live with it.
Fundamental research into the
life of natives. Childish
withdrawal from sensibility. A
form of participation in the world.

Summer Is Almost Over

Summer is almost over
the wall. Music is
slowing down. Ice-cream
doesn't melt as quickly.
Water is too cold. Bring
in the chairs. Light without
a source spreads out in carnal
release. You need warm sun &
cold beer. Fat metaphors
park their sleeping strollers.
Attractive troubled days to be
walking past the hospital,
kicking leaves.

Sun Came Out

Sun came out. What
dazzles us. It relieves
sense of fatality. Stop
decay. Subtle changes in
style. The caress. The old
familiar sun. The new arms, legs.
The new toys. Who was born in.
Choose true objects. Ruthlessness
isn't enough. What a fine uncertainty!

By Night We Played

By night we played on the lawn.
The days were over before we knew it.
A bargain we made. She felt hot
& sweaty in my lap. Tremendous verve.
Memory made of gags. The high shelf
of existing. No one gave up. It can be
as dangerous not to participate.

What There Is

What there is. You
did expect. Why don't
you? Or like that.
The dreams of childhood.
Sand rivers. Climbed a tree
& is successive positions.
The dog wanders inside a factory,
adopts a viewpoint.

When All the World

When all the world is
new. Compulsory credits
should be selected. Pray
to the teaching cobra. Somewhere
between good & dead. To understand
the boredom of earning your worth.
Boom goes a drum. You stand in
the invisible. Eyes are in other cities.

Each Day Has No Limits

Each day has no limits.
Music knocked the pins out
from under you. I enjoy
being alive. The difference
between demand & reality is
tolerated. Two steps at a time.
Frontiers exist to be crossed.
Analysis of the kitchen. Life
is a continent away. The ocean is
so big. You have the day.

History as Long as Time

History as long as time
lasts. The ladies in muslin
in front of their anxious faces.
An early table of contents.
Late afternoon plane landing,
a liberating habit. We wake
& start again. Adjusting glasses,
we stare at aliens. New ideas
in the mind of a draftsman. She
did get the divorce.

Bands of Colour

Bands of colour which
fuse optically into one.
The intelligent dryness
of the leaves against
dead grass. Headlights stare
into the autumn countryside.
We made choices. Our daily
mouths. Smoke in our chests.
A true rendering of the dynamic
movements of confession. Blue
wind in red faces. Not forgetting
the food, nor the music. How
sex swept us into the cafes!
Smashing cockroaches we are prisoners –
but not in Montreal.

Prone Voter

Prone voter. Excited customer.
I am rebellion glued to a
revolving department store.
Current furred socket. Razor sharp
promotion. My mouth
trap flexes wallet lips.

Pastures of Support

Pastures of support in the
parking lot, food city, a
telephone. Throw back the
burger, slow deduction, what
wanted now. Warrior catered
public stride. Mind chewing
property. In the climb through
packages he thought.

Do or Die

Do or die.
Do what you can do.

Glass dust.
Sun blurred in table-top.

Adolescence of repulsion.
Nest curled baby.

Against informal dirt
sky washes chair, table, floor.

Do what you can do.
Nod before heavenly freeze frame.

Into the Exact

Into the exact
hand-painted paradise
packed firm by roaring
graders, the speeding
car flips twice.

A tree. A positive motor
dead. Exalted recognition
of a steering wheel.

Trees on cue
shake their star-filled branches.

I Race

I race to the best
seat in the house.
Mom, pop, the whole
gang. Moon, June,
come rain, come whine.

Spotlight hard as
outdoors, I need
more time, more money,
more energy, to be a blur.

Truant. Regular.
I am going to that retarded
good morning. I am floating
to the side-lines, sensational
arm-chair.

I Am Pulled

I am pulled from lukewarm
water to cooler nipple milk.
Common-sense is yelled into
my tensed ear.

The first building block in my way
is kicked hard, hated.
I listen to the next world
wrapped in the heart of my bed..

I fish for more good wood
at the bottom of a still larger bay.
I feed my temper by sodden diaper,
early bed-time, on the crawl.

No More New

No more new. The road to
home is lined with blood trees.
Burnt-in, elastic, tongue has
sinned against family trunk.
Seeds spill into possessive
observation posts. Stairwells
sweat holidays bumping bellies.

Motion is their meaning. No more
abstraction. The waters of cold
judgement their comfort. Gossip
an obedient employee. Mother, father,
tilt into age. The house leans
& ages me.

The Sum of Its Details

The sum of its details. As
I entered the house. Talking
advice to each successive age.
Steam & potatoes. The outside
disappeared & a stranger. White
shirt parking the car. When I
am leaving. A correction. Emptied
into my plate. Without looking around.

Surprise Us

Surprise us. Paint
the trees. Give in to
your predictable architecture.
Not very musical. Living &
dying. Boring stories. Underground
ocean. The intelligence of dolphins.
Give me the intimate minutes of your
discontent. Career as virtue.

More in Teaching

More in teaching than in
writing. Size of the idea.
Flooded basement. Relaxing
effect of rain. Echoes. Young
anarchists who grow up to be
river-boat captains. Every day
people dying because of some
small detail. Small mushrooms
for dinner tonight. You are
bright as rain.

A Great Fondness

A great fondness for the
common-place. Smudged
pottery. Venice of
shit. To speak of religion
without anger. Old umbrellas.
To sell an idea. She came up
with the right formula. Narrow
hall. high ceiling. Metal
tubing. Hard at work.
To produce no surprises. The
result is a white paper, faint,
ghostly.

As It Appears Every Morning

As it appears every morning. Peopled
with objects. Ironic lucidity in a
crowd. Within favourites. Microcosm
of the whole. Worn thin in a complex
pattern. & revelations denied you.
From a photograph the juices. Not
now. This is very interesting. Never
complete. If we add to this.

Reproduction in Another Medium

Reproduction in another medium.
I remember the outboard motor.
The gasoline on the collie's fur.
Bacon & eggs in those days. A
hardwood jungle. In a sense of
anxious youth. I persisted & swam
to the raft.

New Buildings about Ten O'clock

New building about ten o'clock.
Motionless in the same spot. A
fabulous coincidence. Only the
sound of the waves slapping the dock.
Alarmed, the criminal gives up crime.
Man to distances. That's right.
You didn't help matters. These ambulances.

Stronghold of Non-conformism

Stronghold of non-conformism.
Donate your money to science.
Official propaganda. We own our
houses. You don't want accurate
information. We are generous as
long as you respect our righteous
ignorance. Indicative of a highly
nervous temperament. A grand prize.
Speed of our cars. Everything works.

Some Words Were Repeated

Some words were repeated.
The basic critical texts.
The pottery was blue. A fort
in the woods. Without help.
Proving what power? A cause
of this was our debts. Water
under the money bridge. Collective
humanity. The tree is pregnant.
A reflected image. Died without
pain-killers. Always sunlight.

At Once Perplexed

At once perplexed & full of
hope. The short flight. Up &
down. By all means. It's a
known fact we don't possess
much folklore. A precious taste
for small things. No trouble.
Our vision has been altered.
Bonded by aggression. Thick
happy death. Lacked a clear
understanding.

Insufficient for Our Needs

Insufficient for our needs. Are
yesterday's ideas. Never noticed.
Matches under the ash-tray. On the
road to town. But I don't. We slept.
Little grinning faces. On a curb,
head down. To conquer the world.
Another month. Can't take an endurance.
What to do in this world-class school-yard?

Historic Moment

Historic moment. Describe
that moment with a knife.
You live outside the city. The
weather report wound too tight.
Breathe in the days & nights.
One of the most powerful climates
on the globe. Rescue efforts.
There were no public commissions.
Altar of fresh branches under sun.

Snowflakes

Snowflakes. The
wind. She, old woman,
alone in her house, afraid
of her neighbours. Smell
of chocolate. Much security
obtained. Toward similarity.
I expect you are.

The Emotional Relationship

The emotional relationship
between man & nature. Overwhelmed
by their freedom. Blueberries.
Fantasy made real. Her profile
is heroic. Water warm. Canoes in
the rafters. Wake up hungry.

An Erosion

An erosion of religious
belief. Cliffs are crumbling.
Ice & sand at sensual beach.
Birds resting on the waves.
That school is a launching -pad
to Happy Birthday. Kneeling
& forgiving an obnoxious heart.

Injustice Is on Both Sides

Injustice is on both sides,
dripping with supporters. The
brushwork of explaining facts.
People don't forget. People
are despised. Little fish
at prayer. The dynamic possibilities
of form. To retain the privilege
of elegance.

Anxiety Is Future

Anxiety is future. You'll
leap through the erotic air.
Understand systems & become
an agreeable worker. Respect
for good doctor. Rapture of
guilt. Egg on face. A bitter
excitement. You swim a blue-veined valley.

Not Over Yes Finished

Not over yes finished. Attainable
in use of diseases. One time against
the time. Geese overhead. A series of
humble subjects. Stood outside & then
entered by own key. Pushed into the
subway. I am saying, said.

To Stop

To stop. A growing
appetite for the last
days. Onward & a target.
The law insists. To be
morally correct, Breakfast
that morning. Not true
because of omission. A
very complicated case. To
be altered out of resemblance.
To stop.

Avalanche of Applied Pressure

Avalanche of applied pressure
is digested, shitted.

Praise be away.
Mean what you hear.

Tap fence posts.
Keep your secrets.

Pain the double-checked intestines.
Landscape is your character shake.

President crab enacts righteous applause.
Black & white photographs.

Praise be your miserable god.
Squat up-wind, dignified.

Not Hurting the Back Teeth

For Nicholas, age 2

Not hurting the back teeth,
naked table, routine,
tiles used walked over,
ignored in the present tense.

Clapping laughter. It is:
food cooking, rain not
boring, warm kitchen,
his smiling chin.

A hunger to be on these
fat drops of rain.
Your farther's back cracked,
filled in, smoothed over. Yes.

Eyes in the World

Eyes in the world. Shouts
of a strong family resemblance.
A little bit further in that
neighbourhood producing love
without horror. Dumb in the
perceptive park. Our decisions.
What wanted into & past merry
death. Or something like that.
An old anything. & with that
advantage. Would interest you.
Sit up in bed. As it turned out.
But now that part in depth. What
there is.

In the Process of Moving & Developing

In the process of moving & developing.
Since they are children. A fine sweat.
A rigorous day of physical labour. What's
the use. This is it. Means to an end.
Would be offered with the condition of
loyalty. Has stumbled over the laws of a
nation. Against the obedient class-room.
Much later. Heartless but true. We
headed off on foot. Still they are not
satisfied. To make them comfortable. In
the universe. Grandfather's white shirt
rolled up to his roasted Sunday elbows.
But not by everyone. Inside our routine
complaining. The perfect disaster. What changes!

NEW POEMS

As Much

As much as I
can. Submerge
the constant
tricksters. A
race with great
conquest. Let's
do it, penetrating
clean sugar without
shame. The fabled
view of leisure &
meaning. In a meeting
of chairs, the watchers.
Tolerate on your will.
They are angry & talk
at you. Rush up into
the casual haze. What
I can't have.

The Loss of Community

The loss of community in
a meat cave. I am
bone-brained in my
vital nest of soft
artifacts. Under the
threat of extinction, I'll
hatch a monster or two into
the shouting streets. My
public haunting. I'll
deliver my pumped-up body
into a lemon-sour judgement day.

Temporary & Reactive

Temporary & reactive,
an over-stimulated audience
monitors & applauds. Enjoy
hypocrisy with the advantage
of a powerful police force.
The economic literal machine
motivates & accepts, exploits
& rejects. In the slow-moving
panic are depressed gardens,
stunted trees, rich misery.
You exist in the rigid grip of
honest bean counters. Ants
are swept off the good-life table.

I Arrive

I arrive & feel free
for the first time in
my life. A summer
morning under a blue,
blue, sky. I am not before,
or after, but in my actions.
It is remarkable to soar over
the reasonable decisions. I
do see my demanding ages roam
the skin. I am ready to
be myself in the drenching
vocabulary of to & fro. A leaping dolphin.

Weight of Stones

Weight of stones,
clumps of the past.
A conviction that
my awareness is defined
by others & that is
final identity. Stumbling
run through the too clean
rooms. An old winking statistic
spits on the floor. My
sense of balance waters a
prominent body. I use
open-air techniques. I
shrink to a second. Comfort
stroked. Yes, there. A
transparent curtain covers
future corpse. Brain-pan
sizzles threats to the organized noise.

I Belong Anywhere

I belong anywhere
next to the good-bye.
A willing, active ghost.
What conspiracy? I
am watching myself
spending myself. It
matters. One fast
move in the rounded
city. With every reason
upset. More & less.
Function/appliance bumps
up against heavy traffic.
Urgent bladder. Direct
curse. A profound villain
on the razor-blade of
kind production. O
woeful flesh in the speed!

The You in Blank

The you in blank.
A claw at window
throat. Can't you
understand what
you are doing?
You are spontaneous
& not in danger. A
fixed conceit with
eyes closed. Condemned
in the furious report.
Finished reading. Immortal
with a humble convenience.

Happened!

For my father

Happened! Face stretching,
filling the room. Body
cushion rigid – arching
up in before fear & astonishment.

Closer, the silence of status –
shaking white wood – wet instant statue.
Heavier than air. Stature deflated.

Around & around, at
the joking expense of – whom?
Who is secret, sacred, naked?

Involving over the radar of his
own private eye, destiny, destination.
At once arrested. Gone.

You Are Correct

You are correct. An old,
whiskered heat in earth-cup.
Age deeded to pass elsewhere.
Attractive, balanced, walk. Image
gnawed by regard. It happens.
Worth what hurry? You don't have
action. Go pale cry in character.
Piled clothes, thou stark brow. You,
surely, that must be the case. Single
doubter, mixing. Shoulders rise,
follow in your burial suit. Out.

A Hero Carries

A hero carries wheat into the
arms of security. Tumbles up &
down verb escalators. Misbehaves.
Glows in the snow. Did you see that
bat? Comforted by wrong. You are
scratching & saving for better, best.
The unfair, thrashing, numbing, sea-spray!
Civilians direct sunrise in movie heave. An
unconvinced, massive, not without a struggle.

To Drown

To drown within safety
words. To die within
circling family birds.
To not remain here, like
this. The search for
breath. To see for one
second more. To leave a
trace. That is him.
That is that. A
jumping across safety in
numbers, crowds. Rushed
by, folded up, along
his dried fig body, less there.

Lush Life

Lush life. We do.
I can do this. I
can't do that. A
raw deal. Thin light
on fat trees. Power
of a giver. Sunglasses
beside lunch. They are
careful inside the
puzzling green waves.
As a result, a new trial.
They proceed by the energy
of their applied logic.

A year later & travel
luck & here we are. The
sand is hot. To stride out
of cold water. The soft
games below wet hills.
We examine & stay in
the painting of this pleasure.

In a Crowded Leisure Park

In a crowded leisure park
social mouth chants
hypnotic hymns to joy,
wish, more. Prayers are
skipped across star
lakes of teasing universes.
There is a modest seclusion
found under large, waving,
inheritance trees. Smell
the stink of careful elephants
criticizing peanuts by a gold
fountain. In valid zones
blossom the bouquets of accidental
dream taste. Amen.

In Harm's Strategy

In harm's strategy
slice their bodies
with whirring tv
blades on fast forward.
To turn & fight the
beast. In poised
grandeur roll over
the taunting skull
formations. There is
a language fog. Fugitive
god of disciplined war,
forgive my doubts to
retreat into the wild, cool
computer bombing. Who
receives accurate direction?
Attack & defend with force
& farce. Factual wagging tails
report on moral primitives.
Child is murdered under a
chalk outline inside a liar's history.

Nearby

Nearby. Name & remember.
Return. Retrace your steps.
For experience's sake. Don't
pretend. Pretend. The tender,
curious, finger-tips. A
tooth-pick touch. Repeated
mistakes. To make that
observation for profit, for
fun. Ambitious results with
denial, revelations. Watch
it. Watch out! Can't fly
back. A good impression. A
dog's bark. A solder's
salute. A rapport
with the surgeon. Expose
the consequences like a jack-
knife. The bubble flight
into close quarters. Build the
sleek wings of bargain freedom,
competent reliance. But it
states: talkative, suspicious,
submissive, on your bleeding chart.

You, in Trouble

You, in trouble,
isolated by cynical strength.
A grinning body bed. You
groan thunderstorm in a
freeze, the inside plunge.
Break the hands of Jesus.
My own witness in my
customized shoes. No one
is there. Imagination & pity
locked together in a buried box.

White Tiles

White tiles & a
few black lines.
What he did &
where he went. They
operated on his
heart from the back.

To upset you &
know what is broken
underneath. An insatiable
curiosity, an impacted abstraction.

To surprise, that is impressive.
To invite us in, where it is future.

That Being

That being
said, there
is still another
trembling, startled leaf.

An intimate
shiver with the
logical, knocking doctors.

An intimate
shove for a well-
behaved patient from
the confident routine.

& nearer to the
final, known, landmark,
you are not in control.

Agreeing & Proceeding

Agreeing & proceeding
further into the created
forest, dream, a better
place. Secured, not
abandoned. A worthy arrival.
Not a formal invitation. Rub
each pore. Deliberately
imagined. Visible, slow seconds.
Is this perhaps forever? Days
pile up. On our way. So away.
Got away with us. Are we having
fun yet? Dissident trampoline
jumpers. Body-ache provides a torn
map. A sufferer is witnessed. Is
this perhaps normal progression?

A Gate

A gate. Give meaning
to confusion. His
view of the invisible,
warm parade. No
one dead. The fuel of
travellers in transcendence.
A copy of a later
theme. A strong & serious
smell. I served on
that ship. Delayed in
new environments. Are
yesterday & then what?

I Am Impatient

I am impatient to be
the sensible mercy. Broad,
sensuous, acres of colour.
I am created again, if
being in a pattern solves
my loneliness. The flowers
& trees on its banks. I
am not the enchanted plains
that prolong the arbitrary
particles. I see & hear the
births licked at daybreak.
I'll see what it's like.
I sit in silence & listen to
the water. I am not the tall,
bending grass. Cruel theorist,
I react to rumour in the lower territory.

Catch & Squeeze

Catch & squeeze
damp earth hands.
Nearest roots tell
my story. I leave
the flesh house. I
fall through a closed
window. The expected,
fatal mistake. My
competent administration
no longer rules. Anxiety
in a locked skull-car.
There is too much. Exit.
I am examined by defiant,
cautious, heads. Body
scatters across inland
sea. I am the abstract
diamonds. I am pulled by
waiting hands up to my own ledge.

Chance of a Flurry

Chance of a flurry.
Drone's complaint,
demanding safe passage
from front parlour to
frosted mountain-top.
At the command of foreign
importers. Held by the
hand & calmed down. A
regular group. Cultivate
in the ordinary orchard.
Cows chewing under dry
trees. Morning heat. The
faked confession. He
remained inferior to his
rich customers. Call him
Mr. Logical Jacket. Risked
his reality & knew important
people. Multiply & count cows
in a state of educated responsibility.

I Was Capable

I was capable. I
joined a lawful flight
into reassurance. Fair
& sweet wine. I am
present in these busy
rooms at this time. A
sense of triumph in the
end. & so on. In their
particular sensitive success
I spill my wine loyalty.
To their health. To their
cleaned-up rugs. To their
hard & soft vomit importance.

Gone

Gone from the
cocoon. From
the premises into
nightlight. Do it.
Make history. Keep
the pressure on. Big
moon in your punishing
sleepy hollow. No
free parking. Not so slow.
Never innocent. Amoral limbo.
The same, the always pressure.
I come in, look around, bite hard.

Animal within Solitude

Animal within solitude
before the hello. Reaction
plotted in the elevator.
Where vision sells to a
devious higher-up. Mocking-
bird hill. A maintained
urgency in this experienced
hatred. The vultures don't
panic. A seductive story
as long as the senses are
stimulated. Potent headquarters
blesses itself. Secret &
public, humane wars speed
together, focussed on exact them.

Seekers

Seekers, true believers, ones
who trust the harbour lights,
swerve past me dispensing ecstasy & punches.

Over there, under his laws, our
elect gather at the total shore of salvation.

He is the ocean of loving redemption.
His waves are rolling over the absolute grass-roots.

He is the curling flame/confidante.
His soldiers are killing the blasphemers.

Get on up. External hammer. Praise
the energetic salesmen of intimidation.

Salute your flag. Lock up your country.
God is the needle. You are the eye.

Overgrown with Weeds

Overgrown with weeds.
A series of close-ups.
To be down there. To exhale
a lying reply. So simple.
Face to face. Fine &
desperate. Toward the tormented.
Hidden insect. To deflect a
calm arrogance. The battle is
futureless. A giant's groan.

Stay Inside

Stay inside & never
leave your cabin. See
you later up on deck.
Ship sinks. Here. There.
You know how the wind blows.
Before, a stroll with other
passengers. Bright stains
spreading in the dripping,
building spring. Push someone
else through iceberg down.
Thank you. Wherever it melts.
You are welcome. There. Here.
I arrived, my own slowfooted self.
As a matter of fact, I noticed.

A Continuous Eye

A continuous eye & energy
presentable for centuries in
water minute. Bonedust involved
in every task. Ghost be nimble,
be quick. Monumental hair on
sparkling dinner plate. The
cordial relations between cords
of flesh. As if by speaking, I
am here, neat as a pin-prick. Another look.

Starfish on Neck

Starfish on neck.
let each have their
balloon opinion &
suffer! Home, sweet
jet. Sun-filtered
sofa. Rain a coping
blanket. The knife
against your kite.
Comfort food of cars,
bikes, winding streets.
A rush to trivialize,
spy. Soothing sex
appeal of renovations,
furniture. Dynamic
crime under glass.
What & whom distorted by
a shark media surf.

Media Net

Media net, swaying
sea wall, an infinite
hardware elegance. Not
to be that perfect. Memory
grass slides downhill. At
first chance, burdened by
speculation, I watched the
working legs. A people arguing
up fear. Better streaks of
cruelty, kindness. Neither
possession nor surrender. A
sphere like this. To pronounce
& organize. Recognized by
everyone. Everyone notices my
usual business. Back & forth.

A Flood in My Veins

A flood in my veins.
Is immense. A quiet
evening by the lake.
I immediately am asleep.
Every day within you.
To continue into the acceptable
afternoon. Total cost. Quite
deceptive. Quite imaginative.
Made intent & relaxed. Assurance
at the door. Minutes to waste,
chasing us. Against all constraint.
Keep conscious. What we throw into
air & space. Unconsolable completion.

Eaters Observe Chocolate

Eaters observe chocolate.
You eat a tasty separation.
Fed company, you are that rock,
this engine, that platter of
green & red salad. Famine barge
dredges appetite compass, pleads
hunger. Harvest bowl overflows into
kitchen slippage. Cooked & ready,
you are enjoyed as spice fragments,
marrow broth hot fragrance.

An Intact Room

An intact room. How
lucky I am. An open
fist. I am the shifting
walls. A breaking point
to force the individual.
I race in the running
fields. Remarkable,
punished bodies shy away
from the dead, a night.
Bracketed by guilt, I
want to go past cold winter
windows, tumbling delight.
Not disguise, but clarity beyond
slicing pain. I learn by
my nearness, a human obstacle.

On Church Steeple

On church steeple, I
am under the nub,
added, subtracted.

At the end of busy,
compelling road, I am witnessed
in a silence, responsible.

Any porch town, I slide into,
out of confidence, down main
street, to that obvious intersection.

The Tricks of Recovery

The tricks of recovery.
No matter what I do.
Solicitude of deep mud
under sky-light. A
moment before. Penetrating,
fixated stars. Resisting
jokes on the other side of
face fence. Interviews? Have
I been? Am I going? not
to be fooled. Sustain the
worm-crawl of aging. Respect
the obvious. By repetition
dig a pit in an empty lot.
More intense. Good morning little sunshine.

I Stand

I stand on the stated
beach aiming flat worry
from star to star. I part
the waves to suit my view of
a battle. Righteous answers
spread their hard-earned peacock
feathers. I am the reflex hypocrite knee.

Ah, an emphasis of morality
by the active sceptics,
shifting the roof of blue-black
sky with their strong heads!

So Shall

So shall I survive?
Depth shaved. See
you later? Height
drained. Finger
in ear. Do not
dismiss charity when
it matters. Impose
your blueprint. A
vision of floating
after death. Push the
button on infant scream.
Wary night owl. Quite
distinct. Devastated,
vast continents. You
choose the outcome: operate,
find, die. Minutes smoked
by arrogant lungs, skilled
explainers. Carry me to
the lobby. Morality Play.
Self-conscious. Steps to sharpened teeth.

My Forward Thrust

My forward thrust – a magnified
gleam loud – my highway honk –
squealing spurt inside marketable
my, my, mine only. Higher ferret zig-zags
crumpled cloth-face. Dry sprint thirst.
Dust grain angst re-assembles vertigo slow
brink. My flare red pulse – cranium
clenched against hatching hope. Cloud
giddy jumper. Signature matter aware!

I Am Careful

I am careful with my
conscious, carving, bones. I
jog my cage with available
salvations. I bend & snip piano
wire on the run. I smirk a parallel
universe flapping with smart-ass customers.
Blue & white flags snap in the hot winds
from my interior plain. What burns is
the straw of my one broom. I die forward,
sweating in my noon summer pride. I
dry inside, my own myself.

Void TV

Void TV. I don't
want the angry success
of complete defeat. I
want to stay here in
repair. I'll crawl hope
backwards. An awake investor
orphaned by the conceited
grid. I'll be sardonic twitching
cheek. A sliding glass door
in harmony & debt. The bullet
between friends. A decisive sunset
at once excreted. The tremendous
cuisine prepared by: I'll be, I'll be.

Good & Evil

Good & evil.
Sudden end of
a lucky streak.
Stitch it together.

I do injury. A
hungry, roaming dog.

Many breathers are
involved. Lunging
alligators are sacrificed in the ditches.

You didn't expect.
A cracked egg.
I am no one.

Superb, in the
land of lagoons,
voyeurs, executions.

The Stars

The stars are closer
over an island in
the ocean. Politeness
unto death. A gentle,
warning shove. To
be kneaded into inevitable
bread buy me. Young girl
whirls & hits sister.
Apologetic owner of failure.
The all news life. A
character role has changed
you. To be dangerous in
present tense. Your flexible
energy is an apple in the eye.

Adjusting

Adjusting to a fertile
imagination. As rapidly
as you want. Till the
tears run down your cheeks.
Talk about it later. It
isn't too late to be candid.
Brood on the table manners
of those who enjoy the
consequence of deliberate
breakage. The sharp elbows
in smiling faces. They have
their own agenda. Gestures
& expressions. Honey & branch.
To suit their private purpose.
In their eyes you lose.

For No Definite

For no definite
reason, a slumping,
purifying party. A
roaring fire of hair,
pizza, money, easy boredom.
This is the efficient pepper-
spray & forget. Personal
ambition as a trapeze arc. The
old formal cartoon tossed from
a superior position. March around
an inner circle. The drilled
impulsers do tingle/tangle arid.

This Is

This is an organizer
for a progressive party –
the best solutions are in
tension. To betray &
betray again. What shall
come of it? The nihilistic
prayers savage with belief.
The same measured strategy.
A large stomach. Welcome
at the warm hour. To
mortify the present with
ethics. Gamblers in a
hurry. Solid as a rock.
Accurate as the difficulties
of law-makers & law-breakers.
Familiar efforts to cope
with dignified killers. An immediate
debate. The violent crevice ice
between justice & whacked victim.

Frowning & Irritation

Frowning & irritation
as the rule. I don't
know, but I do care.
Collapsing, struggling,
mares & stallions of
propaganda. In clicking
grief, steps carved under
state pressure. Under fire
& command – people finished,
flying apart. Huge, empty
bunkers guard the heroic
Milky Way. Over mocking
cliffs to be picked up
& shaken like salt –

Domination & Servility

Domination & servility are
wonderful lusts to break inside,
as the mistaken agree to do.

They identify with my respect,
show their own. I am
not interested. Expedient tact.

They burn their ignorant mouths
confessing into my wise, tolerant face.

I, who am never wrong,
weaving my thin social fabric,
as a helpless power broker.

Climb Shame Today

Climb shame today. Rat-face
squeaks tears on heart-couch.
Hand to spleen begs for brain food.
Poor envy yearns for past cries,
songs, calls. I merge with my gasping
clock to bargain more time. My sameday hum.

I Am Tied

I am tied to
a mast in victory.
Where I am not.
I am not patience,
as though you are.
Done this way or not
at all. Reasons to
continue. I am
elsewhere. A difference
to elaborate. I
become everything. I
am a judge, the shadow
on a floor. I stand
& keep leaving the stadium.

The Problem

The problem was not there.
Just yet. To discover an
appreciation of solutions.
A truth which no longer has
the impact. To be refreshed.
It is not intended to be so.
Before words are attempted,
provocative charm. A
finger to the lips. To
pretend to be a magician.
He fell over backwards.
An illusion. It has nothing
to do with any of this. An
instant where you can't go any
further, afraid to vanish.

The Problem Is

The problem is
to kiss & kiss
closed, wet,
lips in the soul
garage. My barricaded
house is at broken-
door peace. Up the
crooked stream I
swim. Paint a fence
red. A world is
singing net-worked
dew. Joking reply:
I am kick-started forward.

Short Flight

Short flight. Are
you evading,
smiling, determined,
as a new question?

You don't know
if you're really
here! They tell you.
Far. Farthest. Farther.

Speak, selective sight.
Salute these articulate
realists convinced by facts!

To Be Noticed

To be noticed &
that is attention.
I stamp the ground,
shake my leg, to
restore circulation.
At the mercy of cascading,
shattered, promises. A
controlled & legitimate
enterprise to defy the
elders, our elastic elites.
Confront bluntly hermit
bird self. To go through
one world flesh beyond sense.
Who mocked & supported me in
my laughing judgements? A hovering
wing's tip, the blind scream.

All Appeared New & Strange

All appeared new & strange
with a lack of blessedness.
Hope's trumpet reduced to a
candled, metallic urbanity.
Find here vengeful dependency
among the useless texts. Futile
work-out of argument & anxious
conscience. Worse than stupid.
Not a shining day. Up at dawn.
Citizens intimate in grievance,
sneezing necessity. December in Summer.

A Privilege

A privilege to
be alive. I
mean to be in
perpetual whistling,
& clean up after myself.
An immediate credible
rebellion & wasted
bright sameness –
come in, stay out.

Except here in the
high afternoon in
a shaded garden.
An un-hurried glass
in motion – I re-fill,
cohere with the
sparrows, for the squirrels.

Terrific, up from straightened
nails, the crickets, the grass.

I Am Applauding

I am applauding
external reality
in a mystery plane,
the emerging cove.
Sometimes funny. A
prayer not a command.
Loud laughing. Eat
for endurance, bruises,
style. No time. The
people around them in
money fat. They have
closed the factory. An
honourable price. Pack
your brain baggage.
Authority by persuasion.
A convoluted design endlessly
rocking. I see more confident
obsessives. Individuals
prayer safe inside their
mushroom walls. A waxed,
staring forehead, house.
What happens: an alert jaw
swallows opinions in the way, in quick-sand.

Sickness

Sickness as critical as
the attitude of suspicion.
A secret canyon. Leave me
alone. Help me. Tied by words.
Contrition. What you'll be.
Declared arrival. On such an
expectation waiting to learn.
When this is finished. What I can't see.

Water pours across the low
country up to my neck. The
rational bridge. To be honest.
To take less. I'll burst at
the seams. Bad. Good.
Bulging force. Both snake & mouse.

About what is expected.
Blurred vowels in an oppressive,
expensive installation. Sonorous
wasp wings. Lethargic ants.
What happened? I mean to desire, say.

The Celebrity Traffic

The celebrity traffic
distracts. They are re-born
on memory's luminous floor.
I have a buyer. Severe,
shining resumes. The art of
the juggler. Uptown. Downtown.
To sink like a stone & be
again. Floodlit facades. Hyped
green grass. An ease of
movement with money, they
who were the power squads in
that time. The drugged culture
to give us invincible. I am
this day & present hole in my
mask. An emergency, muscular
human being. Tough business in
your face. Enough.